T0077888

THA' AMEN IN RECOVERY

ANTONIO A. BURDETTE

Order this book online at www.trafford.com
or email orders@trafford.com

Most Trafford titles are also available at major online book retailers.

Print information available on the last page.

ISBN: 978-1-6987-0391-6 (sc)
ISBN: 978-1-6987-0390-9 (e)

Trafford rev. 11/03/2020

 www.trafford.com

North America & international
toll-free: 844-688-6899 (USA & Canada)
fax: 812 355 4082

I'm going to start off this helpful guide of willingness by quoting one of the good Lords scripture: Are you not much more valuable than they? Look at the birds, they don't plant or harvest or store food in barns, for your Heavenly Father feeds them so unless I'm willing to walk in the likeness of Christ throughout my recovery I can't ask you without asking myself how valuable are you? Question #2: Are you content taking the risk to score the drugs or are you gonna risk getting DUI after DUI such as myself.

By me being a substance abuser I accumulated friends who did what I did and what made it hard to quit when I wasn't around one another seemed to always be in my present to make sure my urge was met I can think back to when I said I wasn't never gonna stop smoking marijuana and then the thought would cross my mind I'm I that far

gone for a dime bag of weed at this point I'm walking in your shoes not wanting to believe that I am an addict so I continue to use it took a day I had just enough to do my laundry then it dawned on me the baskets were the community and the soiled clothes was me as they piled up was I gonna wait for someone to do them for me or was I gonna take them to the laundry mat where I can see the result and start off fresh for me that was recovery.

We can talk all day about who or what got you started using but that doesn't justify if you wanna be clean You have to face the elephant in the room Recovery isn't 30, 40 or 50% its a full commitment to walk in a new light locking away our past of our unmanageable lives which brings me to my third question are you ready for focus.

Focus is the close cousin of confidence without one or the other a successful recovery is still questioned. If you are here because a judge order it's very beneficial to take advantage of his lenient punishment but if you are not willing how will you escape the handcuffs which comply with your urge to use. We have to realize God who is all supreme is not on our level.

Recovery is about focusing on one another experiences with addiction with an open ear as fast as the devil tried to

steal the word sown in the seed immediately Christ listens when you're willing to focus on getting clean its then the savior and your counselor prepare you from back sliding into active usage.

Growing up I knew alcohol was a privilege but I never practice when it came to the consequences that came with it hot days was reason to drink a beer a hard day at work was enough to drink two weekend at the club was reason to drink four or five it all became a self taught habit never realizing the amount of beer my stomach is holding when morning approaches and certain stems of my brain still high.

When you began to focus during recovery you see why its hard for a non-user to look at you as brothers and sisters we all know someone who uses a brother, a sister, a nephew and alot of the time they tend to borrow from someone who don't even use and that's where being focus docs it part cause how long will that last supporting your own habit financially isn't always possible and so you fall in the slump that much harder.

In my opinion dual diagnosis counselors don't get enough credit because the dealer doesn't wanna see a mother get her son back the topics written in this manual

is when your not ready or can't say Amen while in recovery focusing faces you with reality will I be forgiving or can I forgive myself for taking up a hospital bed from someone who really needs one focusing have you asking the questions can I get back the love ones I pushed away.

I've reached this far writing this guide of willingness without sugar coating for once focus on your dealer do he talk to you respectful when you have to find a ride to him bringing more unwanted traffic to his door will he front you the drug when you joining for that hit when the drug alter your appearance do he treat you like you buying large quantities or is he treating you like a low budget junky.

Is he telling you what's being sprayed on the drug to give it a more potent effect or to speed up its growth when you choose recovery you're asking to learn to walk all over again. It takes walking in baby steps to see society for what it is the more time you waste using the more you fall from society likable having a urge whether if its to smoke or drink its just your self taught habit to spend. Spend by handing it back to someone you borrowed from recovery work wonders after you've made progress the mind pushes having urges to the wayside and allows you to feel pleasure

principals such as joy, being humorous, talkative, the things non-users cherish.

We are human and we will make mistakes but don't let a fix close doors in your life I tried to avoid saying this but when they close its over. If you ever heard an ex-dealer talk he brags on him self man, when I was out there I was doing it big but will he ever own up to why cemetaries are pack from gun violence, suicide, over doses again. If I'm choosin' to be Christ-like throughout my recovery I ask you how valuable are you? The war on drugs is simple the doors for which invites us into recovery rotates day in day out again it's a willingful change that the addict has to make some people such as pastors, teachers, even police join together promoting "Say No To Drugs" a great gesture for doing their part.

And others are just spectators watching you fumble time after time feeling like you're happy being the lowest on the todem pole its when you reached that point you tired of scrapping up change. You're tired of pawning your belongings for that small piece of dope in the same manner that your revolving the drug dealer door is the same way you have to revolve the doors open for recovery you have to keep coming 3-4 months in of being clean

doesn't mean you are in the clear. I call it the urging zone because your mind still wanna find out whether your serious or not while attending group we also should wanna know bout putting on the armor of God one piece at a time.

I've walked this walk with you 20 plus years using while on medication. You can never prepare yourself for when that self-medicated cocktail spiral you out of control. Day and night is two different sources when your use to being in that gloomy stage for so long and the first ray of light shines in your face you squinch until you can stand to open your eyes the same as in recovery darkness tries to comprehend light.

The justice system isn't playing bout the war on drugs nor repeat offenders and they're not gonna play patty cake with you the consumer either I'll be the first to tell you sobriety is hardwork but that's it if you say you wanna be clean and you're tired... You gotta put in the work.

Recovery requires being consistent and being consistent means progress and progress means results. You can never make an assessment about a new you if you've always been addicted Feb. 06, 2019 was my last hit of marijuana and I had my last beer I first worried

bout being bored but that later changed when I accepted walking away without having something tangible.

I'm one who believes in making things symbolic such as my cross that I wear and as I attend group I remind myself that I'm wonderfully made and you should strive for that progress to feel the same.

Living as bipolar I now know what's required and what I can furture do to not worsen my progress. Vigils doesn't have to be so often for us if we could just teach them drugs are drugs and medication is two different things and that's based on a psychology level its clearer when you want understanding willingful isn't the key word to sell this manual but its a small word that pack a big punch its a word that the Holy Spirit use for first timers such as myself. But it's up to me to nurture it after he's sown it if it wasn't for my son hugging me throughout the day and telling me he love me my ears wouldn't be trained for group sessions and I wouldn't been able to prepare this to start you off on the right track.

I'm going to bring this manuscript to an end by saying this nothing I've heard in group do I consider ignorance because no one knows why you began using and there's no scientific reason why anyone who never use will try

any drug for the first time not knowing if it will kill them instantly talk about bravery and it is... To take that chance but chances eventually runs out so when you get the urge to use and you make the agreement to get that fix you're the one putting the final nail in your coffin don't just keep chasing after a sensation because your options will began to narrow down will it be the doors of the church holding your funeral service or will it be the door of recovery.

One can say they drink in moderation and if you can hold firmly to that, that's great. But we learn that things can spin-off from drinking in moderation whether its meeting friends at a local watering hole and someone start out buying the drinks or attending a social gathering such as a club or cookout your consumption of alcohol use tend to increase making you more prevelent to the three consequences 1. Jail 2. Impatient treatment or 3. Death the warning labels are all around us but we neglect them each prescription bottle warns us this medication may make you drowsy or dizziness may occur and the alcohol bottle warns us don't drink if pregnant may cause birth defect so when the two are combine daily functions become unstable.

The more you combine the two the brain starts to depend on one or the other for the high that will eventually do long term damage. Again if you can stand firm knowing you drink in moderation I applaud you because drinking ain't the initial problem its abusing it.

For years, alcoholic abuse has torn up families worldwide but we fail to practice avoiding the three consequences and warning signs of when to seek help and the self-medicated cocktail becomes habitual.

In the same manner we teach our children that abstinence is the best protection, we have to teach them that alcohol is a privilege and the consequences that goes along with it. You can be nervous, drug nervous, or PTSD nervous but when you infuse them it can become a problem and not a hidden problem. Attending group has taught me to be true to myself I don't need to indulge myself with alcohol everytime my birthday or holiday rolls around or if I attend any social gathering where its purchase group works and I'm thankful that they are available to correct my wrongs with me by sharing their experiences. I've allowed myself to be torn apart from the natural me and gave dominant control over the me

that would need help in all other areas as I once heard in church their is a spirit that I've allowed to use me.

And the same could be the case with you so I say this find out who it is that you wanna be and make the necessary steps because nothing is bigger than God and my testimony of Jesus is where he's brought me from to where I am now.

As I bring this manuscript to a close I'm going to say this the Lord provided a place just to hear the answer to his question are you not much more valuable than they? Hear my cry unto you by letting Amen in recovery be your final answer.

Alcohol is the ring leader of substance abuse and it's affect that it has on the human brain to manipulate the ability to operate a piece of machinery, drive a gas powered vehicle or do something as simple as cooking. This manuscript isn't a direct target at adults because adults are somewhat experience decision makers. This manuscript is for the developing minds whose motor skills are still in the developing stages. Alcohol has the ability to make one think that he or she is good at whatever it is their doing and yet we have on record that its just a temporary fix while the accident statistics continue to increase.

I wanna go a little further and talk to you about the irreversible side of things damage liver. The excessive usage of the bladder, and kidneys, twitching, and possibly the time consuming usage of Dialysis not everyone you see now a days was born with mental and physical abnormalities. We cause them to become a permanent part of our lives by abusing the drugs, misusing the medication and overdoing the drinking we inflict the damage to our bodies by letting the substances act as normal supplements ruling out Vitamin C, Calcium intake, Carbohydrates the things that replenish the body not to mention "our only body".

People who can't shake this disease called alcoholism and drug abusers chasing after a sensation they will become society public example of being living proof to the naked eye it's so common to see Uncle Pete with his bottle of booze and yet we say nothing because it becomes a sense of normalcy and alcohol claims another one of our beloved family member. You may not think 20 years is long but you can do the math. If you are a cigarette smoker, think how many times you light up just in one day. Nothing stays normal when using these substances it becomes clever enough to brainwash your mobility and further get you to depend on it.

Out of all the tools group session will equip you with. You have to know your triggers. The many things that will refresh your memory on why you need that drink everything from commercials to convenient store posters. They are not going anywhere it's you who has to re-evaluate your way of thinking and put up that wall of resistance and it can be done because I've done it. Sometimes it takes something unexpected to happen to you to open your eyes and if that is the case, hopefully you will live through it to make the necessary changes.

Don't be fool by the stigma of marijuana every bag of weed definitely ain't a good bag especially buying off the streets its been reported that you can take a urine sample or have bloodwork done and whine up with other drugs in your system that you don't even use and that's because the value of a dollar is worth more than the chances you'll get at life in the eyes of a dealer. We have really allowed ourselves to lose focus when it comes to treating people like valuable acquaintances.

We are so quick to offer you a strong drink without asking is there a health problem we can't stand around one another without asking to bum a cigarette if you notice the pack some will even try hard drugs such as cocaine

in the heat of passion meaningfully you become hooked and you'll need money as well as a supplier and I can guarantee you that, that bump won't be that of the first I have to let my readers know I'm not doing this for the driving force of the dollar bill.

It's more rewarding that I can use my hard earned money to document the truth from the street side of things. It would have nearly been impossible for me to put this together if I never experienced alcoholism and substance abuse. When I started using it was with friends and the weed then was good based on how it smelt and the effect it had to make you laugh and later get the munchies. The more I use when we wasn't around one another and the different suppliers I had to get the bag from the effect was different each time and the risk to where I had to get it became a dangerous risk.

It didn't matter how well my name was in these streets I could have easierly been the next victim but every chance that I took and successfully scored the drug I and I alone fed my addiction. I did 20 plus years using drugs that challenged my way of thinking it made it unsafe and risky. And if you're 20 years younger than I and the way chemicals are being used to potent the drug of your choice

you may not be able to bounce back. You don't have to have upfront money or employment to get the required help you need.

Treatment doors and phone lines are always open and that's because they believe in you and one day a clean step by step one day you'll be able to share your testimony sincerely and unapologetic to reach the ones you see. I also would like to add a good book get written on a daily basis and put on the shelves but until a reader picks it out began reading its content its just another book on the shelf and that's my main focus is to have a book of what I know is willingness amongst the therapeutic literature of medicine and spiritual hope.

Drug usage is a difficult act to put beneath you because normally when you tried to achieve something and you didn't succeed, the temporary fix was there to make light of the situation. I want my readers to know I did it. I put that unorthodox misleading self-taught habit beneath me and I could not be happier. "Roses will make a woman smile but a mother getting her child back makes her heart flutter with joy" Even though I hit rock bottom, no one ever told me that I was a loss cause and before you

hear it I would love for you to have read this because you are not the next suicide statistic.

You are not the next 10 'o clock news headline and you are not the next death row inmate to get that overdose. In the process of writing this helpful guide of willingness, I thought that I had enough to publish but I didn't. I had to find a quiet place and ask my savior to lend me his ear that I won't second guess why I want this so badly. Substance abuse is not based on color or your status quo it's a worldwide problem which we unequivocally didn't mind enticing it was the programs I was force to attend.

It was time spent sitting in jail it was my job not seeing my best potential and cut my hours. It was getting evicted and "put out". It was totaling 2 cars due to drinking. It was me allowing my marriage to fail. It was my child low blow concern about my weight. It was the public stares of having bloodshot eyes. It was the loss of a loved one. It was nights my stomach growl and had no money. It was a lack of confidence. It was friends who made using possible. It was my mother losing sleep but mostly it was the church congregation and the power of prayer and anointing that pulled me through. I'm challenging my readers to turn the tables.

I went from "that's a damn shame" to "you are a handsome young man" and every good compliment that you receive will give you the resisting power to continue to get the best results.

Don't let the healthy compliments go in one ear and out the other. I may not have said this to you throughout this manuscript but I have no regrets becoming an addict and carefully I'll explain when something is wrong and you need help to get through it words of encouragement means nothing because your feelings has gain a sensation so words of advice become like 2 magnets compelling against one another.

But as soon as you take that drink, smoke that blunt or cross that line. They tend to trick the brain that they are working together. Easing what could have been pampered with deep meditation but we bypass that because it's about living in that moment.

And now it just feels right when you can own up to being an addict. There's a certain time that you are glad that it happen. Now, I don't ever have to worry about the effect of misusing alcohol and drugs again disrupting my blueprint for a safe living. Sometimes we are blind to the fact the ones who replenish you with the drugs or

the alcohol are not your support, you have to cut them off because it has to start with you. Don't let anyone tells you different. You are ready and you will stand up against those temporary urges to use and let yourself worth shine through under the laws of the Lord Redemption He wants us (addicts) to draw night to him for healing. If we can't due to continual usage, we sooner than later go to be with Him.

And we see that through damaged organs and overdose. Alcohol is the #1 product of self-medicating you either drink for the taste or for the effect whenever you can crush the can and break the bottle. There will be nothing else to replace it with except self-worth. I've always used substances throughout my life and with everything rapidly challenging me, I still manage to listen to my favorite gospel songs in which I felt simply navigated me into a successful recovery. The world that we live in knows quite frankly about drugs and alcohol because in pretty much ever genre of music it's either being glorified or someone's death-defying experiences are used to storyline the whole CD.

I will always have a street mentality and my reason when I had children. I would needed to know their

terminology on what they called the drugs surfacing throughout their band of friends. I'm not the one who does a lot of traveling so I have no choice but to see and hear about what's new drug or alcoholic substance will gateway them into an unprecedented predicament.

I considered myself a very heavy beer drinker if you finish one beer and 4 seconds later you popping the top on another is a real good sign that your tolerance level is weakening. You might one day ask yourself, I'm giving up alcohol and drugs to stand around looking sober while everyone else is having fun that's just it they magnify it as fun and fun always reveal a dangerous side that has a(n) expensive price tag whether you break your arm and a doctor is needed or you wreck your vehicle and accumulate whatever charges.

The judges decides to hit you with It's gonna point you into the debt direction. As each day that I successfully complete my sobriety, I realize that even marijuana being sold in neighboring states are looking for the same thing as any other state. Impaired it's not their way of trapping you it's your deliberate choice to fall victim into the system because of a need or a want which leads me to ask you again, how valuable are you? Only this time can you

except you have been bought with a price in a Godly way rather than the price that's gonna judicially bid you all behind a need or a want.

Allow me to elaborate on over-the-counter and prescription usage. Those pills are manufactured to target inflammation in the muscles and the joints most ingredients we can't even pronounce which tells me that they will do a lot more damage to the organs not needing the attention some pills can thin your intestinal lining. Some pills can thin your blood. Some pills can even cause you to vomit to the point you can't keep anything down to even sustain nutrients. You may never realize you're getting smaller but others will but if everyone around you has a habit who will you take the true confession from.

Seriously I've sat in trap houses moving my bags of weed and watched plenty come in for the hard stuff. Approximately one year later, they see you and speak but you have no clue where you know them from. That's how fast drug abuse can alter your appearance. There are drop dead gorgeous models who was told "I promise this will take away the fear" and whined up living out of hotels and barely making ends meet. Not to mention the weight loss and why her cheekbones are showing. If you have acquired

this manuscript and have read it thus far "Hear my cry unto you STREET DRUGS ARE DANGEROUS take prescription as prescribe and when you no longer ache discontinue its usage"

Your support team should have no use of any substances while in your presence. Only the conspiring dopamine chemical known as Love. I would love for this to reach as many counseling units as possible. This isn't the book that I want to bail me out financially. It's the book of my truth which authorizes that we share a similarity.

MY TESTIMONY OF SHAME

Good evening... My name is Antonio A. Burdette and the reason I've been ask to speak with you because like myself I'm a recovering addict as well as alcoholic

* An adviser is someone who instills in his members values which allows his members assurance and gives them confidence so that they make not the mistakes of venturing into uncharted dangers or becomin' statistics of the streets.

I have a condition which requires the taking of meds to stabilize my thinking and here's why I'm asked to speak with you.

The times when I should have been taking my meds I self medicated I smoked weed, I dranked beer and I've been doing it as long as I can remember friends would

come around and they would suggest lets get some beer or weed and I would follow suit knowing it wasn't gon' agree with my condition.

One night I gather with some friends and we dranked and smoked as usual one friend decided to ride with me on the way home I loss control of my vehicle and struck a telegram pole yes, we both survived I got arrested the moment that I woke up in jail I knew I didn't wanna be there my court date roll around and I had to stand before a man of authority the judge and it took a man of authority for the substances I was abusing to reach me I praise this judge to this day for giving me a second chance at life he didn't wanna hear my excuses he spoke to me as a father would his child and I'm 44 years old.

He made promises to have me locked up and for whatever reason held him back I began listening and thanking him in silence as he seen through me and immediately began scolding me <u>I had to be broken.</u>

So what I'm saying to you is a good natured man doesn't have to be your father to correct you from making the same mistakes you can't always drop your head in shame you have to hold it up and take it and that's the key to receiving what's being said yes you will make

mistakes but let it be mistakes that won't cost you your life or jail time I'mma say this to you because I know you'll understand you don't have to be a saint to teach one another the right and wrongs for a simple living.

I encourage addicts attending group to get involved it doesn't matter how far gone you may have strayed you can make a difference to someone whatever it maybe do something to help someone other than yourself it is truly rewarding and the pay back will be return tenfold.

My name is Antonio A. Burdette and I'm in recovery pushing for a successful life and future.

Printed in the United States
By Bookmasters